# ROBOTS

## FACTS BEHIND THE FICTION

## MICHAEL CHESTER

MACMILLAN PUBLISHING COMPANY
NEW YORK

Collier Macmillan Publishers
London

On title page: F.R.E.D., part of a learning system from Androbot. (© 1983 Androbot, Inc.)

Macmillan Publishing Company
866 Third Avenue, New York, N.Y. 10022
Collier Macmillan Canada, Inc.

Printed in the United States of America
10  9  8  7  6  5  4  3  2

Library of Congress Cataloging in Publication Data

Chester, Michael.
Robots : facts behind the fiction.

Bibliography: p.
Includes index.
Summary: Describes the development of robots, which
paralleled that of computers, how robots work, and the
many functions they fulfill, with emphasis on robots
built by amateur hobbyists.
1. Robotics—Juvenile literature.  [1. Robots]
I. Title.
TJ211.C526   1983      629.8'92        83-61237
ISBN 0-02-718220-7

# Contents

# Author's Note

Once the creations of science fiction and fantasy writers, robots now serve a variety of functions in our complex and technological world, and they are rapidly gaining in importance. In Robots: Facts Behind the Fiction, I examine the science of robotics partially through the creations of amateur builders—computer scientists, electronics engineers, or computer programmers who have built robots out of curiosity and for fun. Because these people have constructed robots in their spare time, they are "amateurs" in the highest and most complimentary sense of that word. Their work has a particularly fresh, inventive, and lively quality, and perhaps that is why I was drawn to describing it.

The book also explores robots produced for the marketplace, but the boundary between amateur robot makers and manufacturers is not that great. Many robot-producing companies grew out of the creative experiments of robot hobbyists. In either case, I have been fascinated by the results of the efforts of a wide variety of robot builders, all of whom have put together some remarkable and intelligent electronic beings.

Naturally, a great deal of technological information goes into the creation of robots, but it is casually presented here so that the reader can appreciate the characteristics of various robots without having to depend heavily on scientific background. Readers who would like to delve deeper into the fascinating technology involved are welcome to investigate the Twenty-One-Statement List on Computer Technology at the end of this book.                M. C.

# Robots and Computers

Robots have been around for quite some time in science fiction—ever since 1921, when Czech playwright Karel Capek coined the term "robot" (from the Czech word "robota," meaning compulsory service) in his play R.U.R. Yet it is only very recently that robots have come into actual existence. This sudden development of robots is due mainly to developments in computer science. It is with the rise of the computer that the story of robots really begins.

Computers are so much a part of our world that it seems hard now to imagine what life would be like without them. What makes a computer so useful, and therefore so widely used, is its ability to do calculations and to keep track of information with a speed and accuracy no human could ever approach.

To do its job, a computer needs a program and data, or information. For instance, consider a program for calculating and printing out all the paychecks for the employees in a large company. The data would consist of each employee's name, social security number, pay rate, and deductions for taxes and insurance. The program would provide instructions on how to use this data to calculate the size of each employee's paycheck, as well as print the paychecks and other records relating to that week's payroll. Some weeks or months later, the data might be very different—some people might have received raises, others left the company, and others joined it as new employees. Nevertheless, the same program would operate on this new data to produce paychecks.

A modern computer can store programs and data in its electronic memory. The program and data are usually typed at a computer keyboard and stored as "software" on a magnetic disk or tape. When a programmer wants the computer to operate on a certain collection of data, using a certain program, he or she feeds the particular program and data into the computer's memory from a disk or tape drive. Once the computer has stored both the program and the data, all it needs is a "run" command, and it does this task at a speed so fast that it is hard to comprehend.

Computers were developed very gradually at first, as various inventors in earlier centuries built calculating machines, using wheels and gears. This process sped up considerably during the war years of the 1940s, when electronic computers were built. These early computers were very primitive compared to even the smallest personal computers in use in the 1980s.

One limitation of the early electronic computers was their dependence on vacuum tubes. A vacuum tube is an electronic control device that looks like a light bulb. Vacuum tubes are not very common today, although they still have some special uses. In the 1940s, however, these tubes were the basis for radio communication and everything else being done in electronics. The most common vacuum tubes were the "diode," which controlled the direction of flow of an electrical current, and the "triode," which could increase or amplify an electrical signal. A combination of diodes and triodes and other electrical parts could take a small radio signal, detected by a radio antenna, and build it up to a power level where it could be changed into sound waves that could be heard through a radio speaker.

Compared to the transistors used in more modern electronic equipment, vacuum tubes were big, slow, and expensive, and they produced a great deal of heat. Therefore, the electronic computers built of vacuum tubes were enormous machines that filled entire rooms. These computers, like the vacuum tubes they were made of, burned up energy, cost an enormous amount of money, and were also slow.

Nevertheless, they were a major step toward the modern computer. They were used to make intricate calculations, mostly for military projects. Not only did they perform these tedious jobs more accurately and with greater speed than humans using pencil and paper, but they were also programmable. That is, a list of instructions could be written and electrically coded for the computer to carry out. Then, data could also be coded into the computer, and the instructions could operate on that data.

These early electronic computers were built at the Moore School of Engineering at the University of Pennsylvania. The first, consisting of a roomful of electronic hardware all wired together, was named ENIAC. ENIAC was programmed through hard-wiring—that is, it was wired together to solve a certain problem, and would then operate on whatever data was fed to it to solve that problem many times over for different sets of data—for instance, calculating the path that would be followed by an artillery shell fired at various different angles with different muzzle speeds and in different wind velocities. But to ask ENIAC to solve an entirely different kind of problem (for instance, to ask it to print a payroll or keep records on the migrations of wild geese) would mean its rewiring.

Rewiring was a slow and laborious process. Fortunately, one of the great innovators in computer science, Dr. John von Neumann, found a way around this difficulty. Why shouldn't the instructions needed by the computer be stored (like the data) in its magnetic memory? With von Neumann's contribution and five years of developmental work, a second com-

The world's first electronic computer, ENIAC. Weighing 30 tons, it filled the entire laboratory with racks of equipment. (Sperry Corporation)

puter was completed at the Moore School of Engineering—EDVAC, which could store programs and data. With EDVAC—although it too was a gigantic, clumsy computer made of vacuum tubes—the computer age really began. This computer could be fed programs and data and could calculate anything it was asked to without having to be taken apart and put back together each time.

Coincidentally, during the same years that the first electronic computers were being built at the University of Penn-

The UNIVAC I, operational in 1951, was the first commercially available computer. Far more advanced than ENIAC, it was still, by modern standards, an unwieldy piece of equipment. (Sperry Corporation)

sylvania, an invention was made at Bell Laboratories that would eventually lead to computers far smaller, faster, and more powerful than ENIAC or EDVAC. This was the invention in 1948 of the transistor. Transistors are small crystals that can do all the things vacuum tubes can do, but at much greater speed, producing much less heat and using much less space.

Since 1948, transistors have become smaller and smaller. Now, as many as a quarter of a million microscopic transistors can be etched onto a chip of silicon (a common mineral) only a quarter of an inch on an edge. These incredibly complex and powerful little circuits are called "integrated circuits" or "ICs" or "chips," and they have made our highly computerized world possible.

There are various different kinds of chips in a computer. One kind is a microprocessor, a chip that controls the computer's logic, performs arithmetic, and generally acts as the computer's "intelligence." Other chips provide memory—the ability to store programs and data—and there are even more specialized kinds of chips in computers. But microprocessors and memory chips are the most fundamental of the ICs on which computers are based.

Even though microprocessors and memory chips are very small, a computer system is usually large enough to use up an entire desk or tabletop. The keyboards, video screens, automatic printers, disk drives, tape drives, and electronic circuit boards that allow people to work and communicate with computers all have to be large enough for a human being to use.

The inner operations of the computer, however, take place on silicon chips, those little square buttons onto which are etched fantastically detailed circuits. The microscopic transistors that make up these integrated circuits operate at incredible speeds, switching on or off in less than a nanosecond—a billionth of a second. (A nanosecond is as small compared to a second as a minute is to two thousand years.)

Although there are other types of computers, the main ones in use today are "digital computers"—computers whose inner logic is based on two possible conditions at every memory location. A particular memory cell can be in an "off" state or an "on" state. This off-or-on condition occurs throughout the entire computer, and, ultimately, it relates to the off-or-on condition of each microscopic transistor in the computer. There are so many transistors in each chip and in the computer as a whole that their off-or-on conditions are as complicated as

Sperry Univac's 1100/90 computer system, introduced in 1982, is a large modern "mainframe" computer. Far faster and more compact than such early computers as UNIVAC I, it also has a much greater memory capacity. (Sperry Corporation)

the pattern of lit and unlit windows in a big city at night. This off-or-on logic is more commonly called a "two-state" or "binary" logic.

Just as they can be put into the Morse code of dots and dashes, letters and numbers can be coded into the offs and ons of computer memory. And therefore, computer programs and data and information of many kinds can be entered into a computer. Some computer programmers work in a binary code called "machine language" made up entirely of zeros and ones that are then changed into offs and ons within the computer. More often, programmers work in "high-level languages" using complex words and symbols that are then translated within the computer into binary code.

All of these developments have meant that there are now fast, low-cost computers that use a very flexible logic. These computers have many vital functions, among which is the operation of robots.

The Lisa personal computer, introduced by Apple Computer Company in 1983. Designed for use on a desk top, Lisa is so much more powerful than ENIAC and other early computers, with their roomfuls of equipment, that it is practically impossible to make a comparison. (Apple Computer Company; photograph courtesy of Regis McKenna Public Relations)

In the early years of computers, an advanced robot would have been expensive to build, would have been big and slow, and would have required comparatively high quantities of electrical power in order to operate. A robot with a built-in EDVAC computer would have been as big as a building and not very intelligent—even for a robot.

However, as the years went by and as computer technology advanced, some fairly clever robots were built. One example was a robot completed in 1969 at the Stanford Research Institute (SRI) in Menlo Park, California. Because of its unstable, wobbling style of motion, the robot was named "Shakey." Shakey was a radio-controlled robot that rolled around in a lab consisting of several rooms with large wooden blocks as obstacles. The robot had vision and touch detectors to help it find its way through this obstacle course, and it also relied on a mental map of the rooms and obstacles. This map was stored in a large computer, which also stored a program that allowed Shakey to interpret instructions from the SRI experimenters, who typed commands at the computer keyboard, telling Shakey to go to certain locations and to push objects together or move them from place to place.

Shakey was an important step in the development of robots, and many later designs made use of the research done on this early robot. But its useful life was short. It was a bulky robot built in the early days of integrated circuits. Even though an improved model of Shakey was completed in 1971, this wobbly robot was finally scrapped in 1973.

Shakey illustrates an important point about robots. The robot's computer doesn't have to be located inside the robot but can be separate from it, with the robot and the computer communicating back and forth through radio signals or over wire cables. On the other hand, many robots in existence today do include "onboard" computers.

There are certain principles common to every robot: it has to be programmable—which means that it has to contain, or be connected to, a computer. And it has to be able to move about or move objects or tools according to its programmed instructions, making decisions based on its program and not entirely on commands sent by a human operator.

Many robots also have "sensors"—instruments that detect light, sound, pressure, and other conditions. The conditions detected by the sensors can be transmitted to the robot's computer to make the robot change its actions—for instance, turning around and going in the opposite direction if a sensor tells it that it has bumped into a wall.

ANTENNA FOR
RADIO LINK

TELEVISION
CAMERA

RANGE
FINDER

ON-BOARD
LOGIC

CAMERA
CONTROL
UNIT

BUMP
DETECTOR

CASTER
WHEEL

DRIVE
MOTOR

DRIVE
WHEEL

Shakey navigates through a laboratory at Stanford
Research Institute. (SRI International)

Since the time of Shakey, robots have come a long way. Now, based on the latest advances in integrated circuits and in programming languages, small, fast, very advanced robots are being built at reasonable cost. There are many reasons for building these robots. To begin with, robots can perform jobs that are unusually hard or dangerous for humans. If a certain kind of part produced in a factory has to be dipped into a vat of acid, it is far preferable that a robot do the job, eliminating the risk to human workers. There are many other jobs that can be done much more safely by robots. It is possible, for example, that robots may eventually be used to paint the towers of large bridges or wash the windows of skyscrapers.

Even in a job that is not especially dangerous—for instance, working on an assembly line—a robot can often outperform human beings. The robot doesn't get tired or bored, doesn't complain about poor working conditions or need to take a lunch break or a vacation or call in sick. It is therefore often more practical for a manufacturing company to program robots for certain jobs instead of training people to do them.

This has raised some very difficult questions. If a single robot can do the work of several people, then what will those people do for jobs? Some experts in robotics fear that robots will cause even worse unemployment, while others believe that the use of industrial robots will create more jobs than are taken away. As they see it, many new factories will come into existence just to build robots. New kinds of jobs will arise— more skilled positions, such as programming robots or testing or selling them. Also, they argue, if conditions in industry are improved through the use of robots so that companies in general are more successful, there will be more jobs for everyone. Furthermore, as robots take over the most dangerous and exhausting and monotonous work, people may be freed of a burden—far from being unemployed, they will work shorter hours and at more interesting kinds of jobs.

It's not obvious yet who is right. Similar questions arose in the Industrial Revolution of the nineteenth century when skilled workers who used hand tools felt threatened by the sudden buildup of machinery. Computers themselves have prompted similar worries—especially when a computer can process information faster and more accurately than a whole building full of clerical workers.

In any case, for good or bad, computers and robots are here, and it remains to be seen what effects they will have on the quality of people's lives.

Aside from the practical uses for robots, there is another

reason they are built. People are curious. They want to see what they can do with computers and machinery. And they are curious about robots and how in time robots may develop and whether robots could ever become truly intelligent.

This creative and playful urge just to see what can be done has always been one of the main forces—perhaps the single most important force—behind progress in science and engineering. It's part of the urge that makes us want to explore the world around us and play a part in shaping it.

Whether this creative activity by the builders of computers and robots will lead to real artificial intelligence—electronic "life" that can really think like a human being—is not something everyone agrees on. Can a machine have feelings or common sense? If it doesn't "want" something, if it doesn't laugh, cry, or love, feel happy or angry or sad, then it seems that a computer or robot could never have the motivation to learn and grow on its own, no matter how much intelligence was built into it. It's hard to imagine that a robot could be driven by the creative urge to see what it could build. Yet, it is still very early in the age of robots, and there is much we don't understand about nature and science and intelligence.

For the present, everyone is agreed that computers and robots as they are today and as they will be in the near future are not intelligent in the same way that human beings are. The inventors who build these systems generally realize that they are imitating human intelligence in their creations. And when they describe a robot as "truly intelligent," they are perhaps partly having a little fun with the idea.

It is very natural to react to a robot as if it were an intelligent living thing because it often acts so much like one. People who work with robots often describe them as "seeing" something with their light sensors, "feeling" something with their pressure sensors, and "knowing" or "deciding" something with their computer logic. Actually, this is a useful way of talking. It is much simpler to say that "the robot sees the table" than to say "the robot's light sensor detects the table."

# A Robot Named Timel

Many of the most interesting robots today are being built by private persons rather than by companies. The people who do this are hobbyists or researchers interested in trying out new ideas concerning computers or computer programming. One of these experimenters is John Blankenship, who is also a professor at the Devry Institute of Technology in Atlanta, Georgia. His robot is named "Timel." The name comes from the first letters of "Truly Intelligent Mechanical Electronic Life." Blankenship built his robot as a software experiment—to explore the ways in which computer programs could be used to create an intelligent robot.

Professor Blankenship made Timel in his spare time, and he found ways to do this at very low cost. The robot's body is made of cardboard panels that were cut out and then taped and glued together. Later, Professor Blankenship strengthened this shell by adding layers of fiberglass cloth soaked in resin. Finally, he sanded and painted the entire shell to complete the robot's body.

Timel's head is an upside-down fishbowl that has been spray-painted to make it solid looking, although, when an inside light is turned on, the entire head glows. The lid of a glass candy jar is perched as a cap on top of the head.

Timel has a single arm. This arm can bend at its shoulder, elbow, and wrist. Notice the photograph of Timel, which

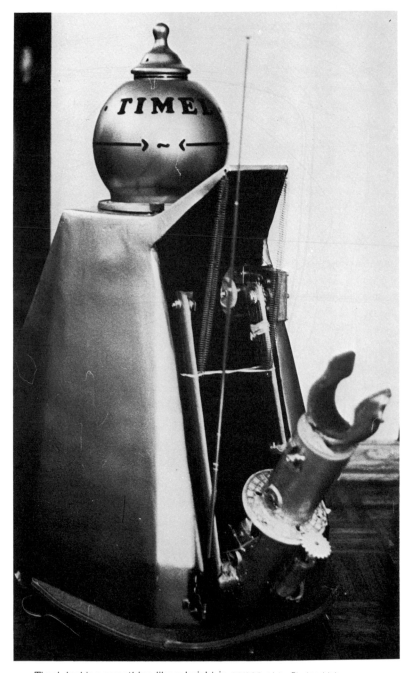

Timel, looking something like a knight in armor. (John Blankenship)

shows the mechanics of this arm, with the shoulder joint at the top and the elbow joint at the bottom. At the end of the arm is a hand made of two pinewood pincers that can grab things. Professor Blankenship also made this arm out of simple materials. For instance, the wrist is an empty potato-chip can with the top and bottom removed. A little motor at the wrist turns a cam (an irregular-shaped piece of wood) to make the hand open. When the motor turns a little further, a spring pulls the hand closed. Timel has three wheels and can roll around as well as pick up objects.

One of the nice things about Timel is that it is a small robot, less than three feet high, and easy to transport. When Professor Blankenship wants to take the robot somewhere, he takes off its head, loads the body into the car beside him, fastens a seat belt around it, puts the head in the back seat, and drives to wherever he is going. When he arrives, all that he has to do is take the robot out of the car and put it back together again.

Timel has three "brains." One of these is a KIM I single-board computer mounted inside its body. The other two brains are outside Timel's body and not even connected to the robot. The second brain is a model airplane control box that can be hand operated. The third brain is an Apple II computer.

Let's see how each of these three brains operates to control Timel's motions. To begin with, the KIM computer inside Timel receives instructions from the model airplane control box, telling the robot which way to go and when and where to reach out to pick something up. The control box is hand operated—and if that were all there was to Timel, it would not be much of a robot at all. Instead, it would be more like a radio-controlled model airplane.

To be a true robot, Timel has to make decisions on its own, using its computer program and also the information it gets from sensors. Timel is a fairly simple robot and has just a few kinds of sensors. To begin with, it has a sense of touch. It has bumpers, something like a car's, and when one of these bumpers hits something—for instance, a wall or a chair or the family dog or someone's leg—small pressure sensors mounted on the bumper immediately turn off the robot's wheel and arm motors. Other pressure sensors mounted on Timel's overhead radar antenna will turn the motors off if the antenna bumps any overhanging obstacle.

This reaction by the robot is completely independent of the radio control signals being sent to it. Someone operating the control box could accidentally give Timel a signal that would send the robot crashing into a chair—but Timel would refuse that signal and turn off its motors as soon as it felt pressure against its bumper. This reaction is to protect Timel from being damaged rather than to protect nearby people and furniture. Timel is not a heavy-duty robot. It is lightweight and even its handgrip is gentle. About the most damage it could do would be a small scratch in the wall paint.

Its owner is planning to improve Timel by adding an ultrasonic sensor. This sensor will use sound waves too high pitched for the human ear to detect, and these "ultrasonic" waves, bouncing off walls and other objects, will let Timel know about a possible collision before its bumper makes contact.

Timel has another kind of sensor. The robot senses when its arm is near the end of its reach or if its elbow or any other joint is bending too far. The robot prevents damage to its arm in these situations by shutting off the arm motor causing the problem.

Except for these safeguards, Timel obeys the radio commands. To command the robot from the model airplane control box, the user operates a pair of levers called joysticks. One of these has been programmed to control Timel's wheels and direction of motion. The other joystick controls arm and hand motions.

In the third method of operation, the Apple II computer is hooked up to the control box. Then the box is operated electronically by the computer instead of by motion of the joystick.

In order for a computer to "tell" a robot what to do, someone has to write a program. Professor Blankenship's programs, written for the Apple computer, give Timel routines of where to move, when to reach out to pick up something, and everything else about its motions. The program is written in a popular programming language called "BASIC," is entered into the Apple II, and then the computer can send Timel on various kinds of missions, rolling around the room and picking up things.

In this situation, it is as if the Apple computer is Timel's "brain"—the only peculiar thing being that now Timel's brain is located outside its body. The computer program is a sort of higher intelligence directing Timel's motions. But the robot still uses its built-in computer, the KIM, as a simpler kind of intelligence that will block the commands from the Apple when they lead to trouble.

People have lower levels of intelligence, too. Your eyes blink automatically if something moves quickly toward them, and if you touch something hot, your hand pulls away even before you know that you are being burned. These simple, protective reflexes have the advantage of being very fast in a situation where there is no time to think.

In the same way, Timel, imitating a human being, has its higher intelligence in the Apple—but it has fast-acting reflexes in the KIM I that operate on their own.

Timel is a simple robot, but it has a kind of cleverness that makes it almost like a living thing. Other robots that will appear in this book may be more complicated or designed to do more serious jobs, but they are all like Timel in many ways. They use programmed logic to make decisions based on what their sensors tell them, and these decisions then control their motions.

# 3

# Robot Tortoises and Robot Turtles

One of the earliest robots ever built was designed in England in the 1950s by a scientist named Dr. W. Grey Walter. Because of their shape, Dr. Walter called them "tortoises" and named them "Elmer" and "Elsie." He built two of the tortoises, each of them equipped with a bowl-shaped shell, four wheels, and two battery-powered motors—one for powering the wheels and the other for steering.

Dr. Walter was the director of a biological research institute in Bristol, England, and he built his robot tortoises in order to help him to understand the reactions of animals and people. These imitations of life, as he called his tortoises, were designed to provide clues about how the nervous systems of living things work.

At that time, there were no integrated circuits etched on silicon chips—those hadn't been invented yet. And, even though transistors had been invented, they weren't being used yet in computers. So the onboard computer Dr. Walter designed for each of his robot tortoises consisted of two old-fashioned electronic vacuum tubes that were about the size of light bulbs.

Each tortoise had two kinds of onboard sensors. First, it had a flexible ring mounted around the edge of its shell that would act as a sense of touch if the tortoise bumped into an obstacle. Second, it had a light-detecting photoelectric cell mounted on a stalk at its front end. Also, there was a hutch in the laboratory that served as a home base for the tortoises. It had a beacon light at its door and an automatic battery charger inside.

When one of the robot tortoises was turned loose, both its drive and steering motors would be operating. This combination of motors would make the tortoise wander around in a twisting, looping path. This was known as its "search mode." When it happened to turn in the direction of a light, its front-end photocell would detect the light and would send a signal to the onboard computer. The computer would then shut off the steering motor, and the tortoise's wheels would automatically lock in that direction. Since it would be aimed at the light when that happened, it would head toward the light. This was its "homing mode."

However, certain events could interrupt the homing mode. If the light were turned off, or if the tortoise veered so that it wasn't seeing the light, the computer would turn on the steering motor, and the tortoise would go back into its search mode, circling and twisting from place to place until it again saw the light—or saw some other light.

It might sound as if this ability to head toward a light would make it easy for the tortoise to see the beacon light of its hutch and head for home. But Dr. Walter didn't want the tortoise to go into the hutch until its batteries needed recharging. He found a clever way to accomplish this. He built some logic into the tortoise that made it turn away from a light if the light became very bright.

When the tortoise, with its batteries still strong, came very close to the beacon light of the hutch, the light would appear very bright—just because it was so close. So the tortoise would go back into its search mode, automatically turning away from the light.

This would happen over and over again. The tortoise would approach its hutch, get too close, and then wander away from the bright light. As it wandered, it would be in its search mode, and sooner or later it would see the beacon and head home again. So this puzzled creature would spend its time heading toward the hutch and then going away from it over and over again.

Then, finally, the tortoise's batteries would start to run down. Because of the weak batteries, all lights would look dim to the tortoise—even lights that were very close. It could therefore go all the way up to the beacon light and into the hutch without being driven away. Once inside the hutch, it would be recharged automatically and would be ready to go wandering again.

Dr. Walter later improved the robot tortoises in various ways. For instance, he added a small light to the top of each tortoise's shell. The tortoise couldn't see this light itself, but Elmer and Elsie could see each other's lights, so they would approach each other and then steer apart, going into strange little dance patterns as they went back and forth between their homing and search modes.

Even though these robots used very primitive electronic computers, they were cleverly designed. Many of the ways in which they operated are used by advanced robots today.

Meanwhile, the idea of robot tortoises didn't disappear. "Tortoises" made a comeback years later as "turtles" when, in 1979, William D. Hillis, a college student who was studying artificial intelligence at the Massachusetts Institute of Technology (MIT), designed a robot turtle with a transparent shell 3½ inches high and two wheels almost large enough to fill the shell. The entire shell was a collision detector, and when the turtle collided with something, the detector signaled the on-board computer, which then sent the turtle on a new path. So far, that was very much like the earlier tortoises.

However, the turtle could do something else. It had a pen it could lower, and it could draw the path it took, so that later on you could see exactly where it had gone in its journeys. It also had the ability to store all its motions in its mem-

Two turtles working together. On the display screen of the Apple computer the LOGO Turtle (the small white triangle at the bottom of the screen) draws a pattern. Working on the tabletop, the Tasman Turtle draws the same pattern on a sheet of paper. (Terrapin. Inc.)

ory. Then, after it had wandered around for a while, it could be commanded to draw a picture of its route, in reduced size, on a sheet of paper. It could even be sent into a room, where it would wander about, bumping into walls and furniture, and then draw a fairly good map of the room, showing where the walls and pieces of furniture were. This little robot was one of the first to be offered for sale as a home robot, by a company called Terrapin, Inc.

But something else had been happening at MIT in the years between Walter's tortoises and Hillis's turtles. A new computer language named LOGO had come into existence, which depended on a little "turtle" that moved across a computer display screen. This turtle wasn't a robot nor even made out of hardware, and, in fact, it didn't even look like a turtle. It was just a moving shape on a screen, a small white triangle with two black dots for eyes.

The LOGO language was initially invented in the late 1960s to help elementary school children and other beginners learn computer skills. The way the language worked was that the person using the computer could order the turtle to walk in different directions on the screen. Then, as the turtle walked, it would trace out letters, numbers, geometric shapes, and so forth. Eventually, it became obvious that such a good computer programming language would also be useful in more advanced applications in education and science. So LOGO grew up to be a powerful language used by professional programmers as well as learners, and it is still growing.

Even though it wasn't a robot but only a shape on a screen, the LOGO turtle eventually became involved with robots. Here is how it happened. A company named Flexible Systems of Australia developed a robot called the "Tasman Turtle" that was similar in many ways to the Terrapin Turtle. Meanwhile, the Terrapin company, which was redesigning its own turtle, entered into a business arrangement with Flexible Systems to market the Australian turtle in the United States.

Another idea occurred to the people at Terrapin. Why not use the LOGO language along with the Tasman Turtle to build a complete turtlelike educational computer system? The system was built, and the photograph shows how it operated. The LOGO Turtle is drawing a line pattern on the screen of a computer terminal. At the same time, the Tasman Turtle is drawing the same pattern on a piece of paper on the table.

# 4

# Robot Arms

In science fiction or fantasy, a robot usually has an imitation human body with arms, legs, and a head. Actual robots have only those parts they need to do their tasks. In fact, many robots are nothing but "intelligent" arms.

This emphasis on robot arms grew from the fact that the most practical use for robots is as workers in manufacturing tasks. This can mean doing welding jobs, spray-painting, loading and unloading parts into furnaces, doing assembly work, and loading and unloading heavy equipment between carts and work areas. All these activities require the ability to grasp, lift, and manipulate objects. To do these things, a robot doesn't need to walk or talk but needs a strong, flexible arm. And, if all it needs is an arm, it might as well be an arm and nothing more.

To be useful, a robot arm must move very much the way a human arm moves. It has to be able to reach out, lift objects, move objects from place to place, twist bolts and nuts, or do other familiar actions. So robot arms are designed as imitations of the human arm. They have joints that are like shoulder, elbow, and wrist joints, and they have hands that can open and close and grasp objects.

Some robot arms were developed as small experimental or training models. Arms of that kind are useful for a manufacturer who would like to try out different ways of using robot arms before actually investing in heavy-duty arms and installing large numbers of them in factories. A small arm is also a good way for a programmer or a robot hobbyist to start learning about the possibilities of robot arms and how to work with them.

One example of an experimental robot arm is the Mini-Mover 5, made by a company named Microbot. The Mini-Mover 5 is not very big. It has a reach of 17½ inches and is designed to stand on a tabletop. It has four joints. One of these is a universal joint at the base that allows the entire arm to swing in an arc, like a crane or derrick. Next are two joints in the arm that act like elbows because they provide for hingelike motions. Because of its position, one of these elbowlike joints is called the "shoulder," and the other is more

MiniMover 5 in action. (Microbot. Inc.)

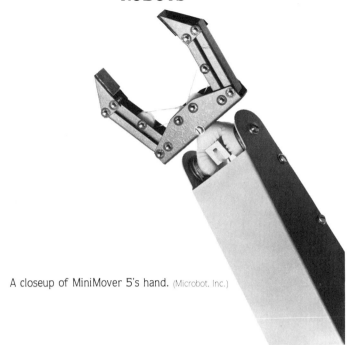

A closeup of MiniMover 5's hand. (Microbot. Inc.)

correctly called the "elbow." Near the end of the arm is a "wrist" that can bend and can also turn—the way you would turn your wrist to twist the lid off a jar.

Altogether then, MiniMover 5 has five possible kinds of motion—rotation at its base, at its shoulder, at its elbow, and two kinds of motion at its wrist. These five motions are what give MiniMover 5 its name. In scientific language, the arm is said to have "5 degrees of freedom" in its motions.

At the end of the robot arm is a gripping hand that has two fingers. Using this gripper, the arm, stretched out to its full length, can lift a 1-pound weight. The speed at which it can lift an object is anywhere from 2 to 6 inches a second, depending on the weight of the object. The hand can open to a width of 3 inches and can squeeze with a force anywhere between 0 and 3 pounds.

MiniMover is connected by an electric cable to a computer that acts as the robot's brain, sending commands to the arm. A special language called "ARM-BASIC" is used to program the computer to make the arm carry out different actions.

Standard computers can be hooked up to the arm—either an Apple II or a TRS-80 can do the job.

A sample of what this robot can do was shown in a chess-playing demonstration. This was not a case of computer chess in which the computer uses its intelligence to calculate its best move. Instead, an actual world-championship chess match between chessmasters Bobby Fischer and Boris Spassky was enacted by two MiniMovers that were programmed to move the chessmen as Fischer and Spassky did in their match. This meant that the computer program that controlled the two robots told each one when to move, where to reach to pick up a piece or pawn, and where to move it. Instead of being an exercise in chess playing, it was an exercise in moving small objects accurately from place to place.

Two MiniMovers "shake hands" before reenacting a chess game. (Microbot, Inc.)

For the two MiniMovers to make the right moves, the chessboard and the chessmen have to be accurately placed because the instructions from the computer tell each robot where to reach to find a chessman. If there is no chessman in the position where the robot grabs, it won't grab anything but air. However, if the robot does miss the chessman and grabs only air, pressure sensors in its hand tell it that it isn't holding anything. Then, error signals are sent back to the computer, and the computer stops the motion until someone can adjust the position of the board or the chessmen.

Although MiniMover is mainly an experimental system, these same kinds of instructions can be used for practical purposes—a MiniMover can be programmed to move parts from place to place in an assembly-line operation, to assist in manufacturing products made from small parts. It can also be programmed to produce computerized art, using felt-tip pens or paintbrushes.

The obvious way to build a robot arm would be to put motors at all the joints. If MiniMover had been built that way, it would have one motor for each degree of freedom—two at the wrist joint and one at each of the other three joints, as well as one in its hand. Then these motors would operate under computer control to bend the joints and turn the wrist and open or close the hand, depending on the command given. But the weight of these motors would be a problem, especially with the motors near the end of the arm at the hand or wrist joint. You can find this out by holding a weight of a few pounds close to your chest, and then holding that same weight out at arm's length, which is far more difficult.

The same would be true for a robot. All that weight would require an elbow motor much larger than the hand and wrist motors to move the heavy "forearm." Working back toward the base, each motor would have to be bigger and more powerful. The result would be a heavier, more expensive robot.

The designers of MiniMover 5 avoided these weight problems. Instead of putting a motor at each joint, they put all the electric motors at the base of the robot arm. Cords run from these motors to the joints they operate, by means of pulleys. Except for the pulleys, this is similar to the way a human arm works, with muscle tendons as cords. Imitating the tendons of the human body is not new. For many years, airplanes have been controlled by cables that operate the tail assembly and ailerons.

MiniMover's motors are "stepping motors," also called "stepper motors" or "steppers." These are electric motors that turn on and off very rapidly so that they make many small partial turns instead of spinning continuously like most electric motors. This motion is like the motion of the channel selection dials of some TVs, which, as they are turned, click to a stop at each channel. However, the stepper motor spins so fast that someone watching it wouldn't see it stop and start, and the joints of the robot that are controlled by the stepper seem to move smoothly.

There are real advantages to this on-and-off motor action. The main advantage is that the series of on-off moves is very easily and exactly controlled by a computer as it sends out a single control signal for each small step the motor makes. This step-by-step logic is very natural for a digital computer, since its own built-in electronic logic also works in a series of steps. There are also some disadvantages to stepper motors, as will be discussed in the next chapter. Some robot builders have chosen one approach and some have chosen others, depending on the whole design of the robot and the ways in which it is to be used.

After designing MiniMover 5, the Microbot company produced a later model that is a lot like MiniMover, but with some special features. This robot arm is named "TeachMover."

Instead of writing a program for TeachMover and turning over control of the robot to a computer, the user operates TeachMover from a control box. On the box are command buttons that tell the robot what to do. When it is operated in this way, it is not really acting as a robot but rather as a machine under human control. But if a RECORD button is pressed after each instruction, the instruction is saved. Finally, after TeachMover has been put through a long series of moves

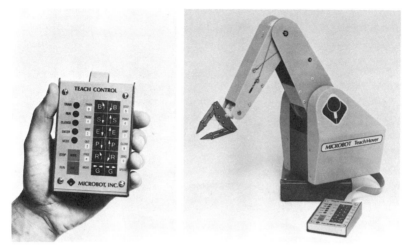

TeachMover has a design based on MiniMover's, but adds a learning capability. (Microbot. Inc.)

(which are recorded), a button can be pressed that makes TeachMover repeat all the motions that it has been led through. In other words, the controls can be used to guide TeachMover through a series of actions it can then remember. By giving TeachMover this ability to learn, its builders were intentionally making it similar to some of the most advanced robot arms being used in factories, which also have this ability.

MiniMover and TeachMover are generalized robots that can be given many different kinds of lifting and moving jobs. However, some robot arms are specialized to carry out only certain tasks. Arms of that type are said to be "dedicated."

Some dedicated robot arms have been built for the one and only purpose of playing chess. One example of this is the Robot Adversary, a chess-playing arm made by a company in Hong Kong called Novag. This electric arm has three grappling fingers that enable it to pick up chessmen and a shoulder-and-elbow action that moves each piece to a new position.

The Robot Adversary includes a special chessboard and

The Robot Adversary makes its move. (Gavon Corporation)

chessmen. The robot arm and the chess set are all part of a single system, with the arm mounted at the edge of the board, as shown in the photograph. Actually, the chessboard is a computer that can look ahead in the game to calculate its moves. Through sensors under the board, the system can detect the location and moves of each chessman and keep track of all moves.

An earlier chess-playing robot named "Boris Handroid" was also designed as a combination chessboard and arm. Boris was given the ability to speak as well as to play chess. When capturing an opponent's piece, it could say, "Too bad." And, when learning from its logic that it had won a game, Boris Handroid could ask, "Ready to resign?"

# 5

# More Robot Arms

MiniMover and TeachMover, with their electric stepper motors and their cord-and-pulley arrangements, represent one of many different kinds of robotic arm. A different approach is illustrated by the Rhino XR-1, another tabletop arm that has a lattice-looking structure like a derrick.

The XR-1 is also an experimental model, but it uses continuously spinning electric motors called "d.c. servo motors." The "d.c." stands for "direct current," meaning that the motor gets its power from a steady electric current, like the current from a battery, rather than from a rippling "a.c." or "alternating current" such as the current from a wall plug. (The a.c. current from a wall plug can be changed to d.c. by a transformer for many purposes, including operation of robots with d.c. motors.)

A servo motor is self-correcting. The motor sends signals to an electronic "controller," which is a simple computer specialized for doing a certain control job. The signals tell the controller the speed of the motor and the instantaneous spin position of its spinning shaft. Then the controller, using a program that specifies what the motor speed and spin position should be at each instant, sends correction signals to speed up the motor or slow it down.

Most electrical robot arms use d.c. servo motors. Even

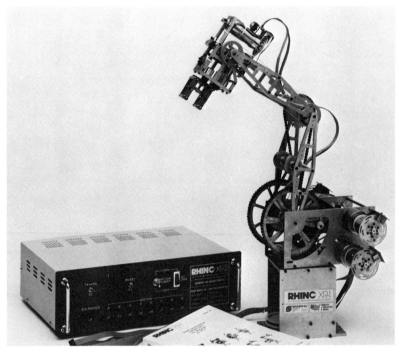

The Rhino XR-1 (Rhino Robots. Inc.)

though, compared to a stepper, this kind of motor is more complicated to computerize, it allows for smoothly varying corrections.

Besides having d.c. servo motors, the Rhino XR-1 is different from the Microbot robot arms in another way. Instead of using cords and pulleys to transmit the motions from its motors to its arm joints, it uses gears and chains, like a bicycle. This design leads to a less flexible but stronger arm. However, for its hand motions, the XR-1 uses a cord and pulley.

The Rhino company has built another robot arm, the Rhino Charger. The Charger is a bigger arm than the XR-1, designed for industrial tasks but using the same basic design as the experimental XR-1.

There are many robot arms not run at all by electric motors. One alternative is a "pneumatic" arm run by the power

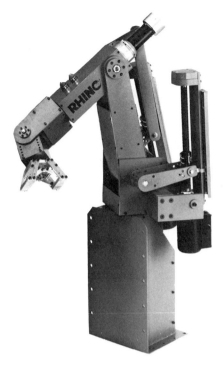

The Rhino Charger is an industrial arm with six degrees of freedom. It has electrical d.c. servo motors to move its joints and an air-powered hand. (Rhino Robots, Inc.)

of compressed air. Electricity is used to run the air-powered motor, and electrical signals from a computer or controller still provide intelligence. But compressed air provides the power that directly moves the arm. Therefore, this kind of arm has to be attached by hoses to an air compressor.

Air-powered arms are very fast acting and comparatively inexpensive to build. But they are not very powerful, and they don't have the precision of either the stepper or servo d.c. electric arms. Air-powered arms are good for lightweight industrial tasks where speed is important.

An example of an air-powered robot arm is the Motion-Mate from Scovill, Inc. MotionMate uses a telescopic type of motion, as many air-powered robots do. It rises up from its base (like a grease rack in a gas station) to a programmed height, then swings around (like a gun turret) to point in a programmed direction. Finally, the arm telescopes in or out to reach a programmed location. These three motions (up or down, turn, and reach) can put the robot's gripper anyplace in the local vicinity. It has 5 degrees of freedom and can swing completely around on its base to point in a reverse direction in one second. It can rise to a height of 3 inches above its base, can reach out to a distance of 1 foot, can turn its wrist joint, and can grasp objects in its hand.

Seiko, a Japanese manufacturer, has built several models of air-powered robots. Since Japan has put more robots in its factories than any other country, Seiko and other Japanese companies have been very busy in robotics. The air-powered Seiko robot arms include models 100, 200, 400, and 700. Like many manufacturers who produce more than one kind of robot, Seiko also makes electrically powered robotic arms.

Another type of robot arm uses hydraulic or fluid power. In many ways, hydraulic arms have the same characteristics as pneumatic arms. That is, they are fast moving, less accurate than electric robots, and tied by hoses to a compressor. However, there is one major difference. The hydraulic robots are very powerful—more powerful than robots with electrically powered arms.

Unimation, a robot manufacturer in Danbury, Connecticut, builds a series of hydraulic robot arms known as the "Unimate" series. The strongest of the Unimates can lift a weight of 450 pounds. At first, this may not seem impressive compared to a human weight lifter. But the robot can lift 450-pound weights all day long at full arm's length and in fast motion.

It's interesting to compare this with Unimation's electrically powered PUMA robot arms. The maximum weight a PUMA can lift is 22 pounds, which means that it is only about one twentieth as strong as a Unimate. However, the PUMA is also about twenty times more accurate than a Unimate. This kind

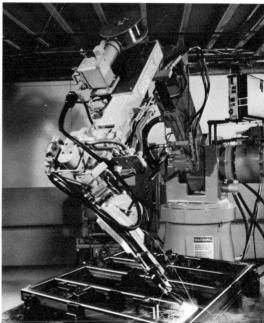

Above left: MotionMate (Schrader Bellows Division. Scovill. Inc.) Above right: The Seiko M700 (Seiko Instruments. U.S.A.. Inc.) Below left: A Seiko M700 feeds parts into a machine. (Seiko Instruments. U.S.A.. Inc.) Below right: The Cincinnati Milacron T³ doing a welding job. (Cincinnati Milacron)

of contrast is typical when the stronger hydraulic arms are compared to the more accurate electrical ones.

A real powerhouse in robot arms is the Model FC from Prab Conveyers, a company in Kalamazoo, Michigan, which specializes in hydraulic robots. Model FC can lift a ton (2000 pounds). Another well-known family of hydraulically operated robot arms is the 500 series of T³ robots from Cincinnati Milacron. The strongest of these can lift 225 pounds. Electrically powered T³ robots (series 700) can lift as much as 90 pounds, which is impressive for an electrical arm.

ASEA, a Swedish company, makes electrically powered robot arms that use neither cords and pulleys (like MiniMover

Unimation's small industrial arm, the electrically powered Puma. (Unimation, Inc., Danbury, CT)

Two examples of Prab's Model 5800 robot loading and unloading parts into machines. (Prab Robots. Inc.)

The big ASEA IRb-60, which can lift 132 pounds. (ASEA Robotics, New Berlin, WI)

or TeachMover) nor chains and gears (like the Rhino XR-1 and Charger). Instead, the ASEA robots use a very strong linkage made of metal rods, some of them threaded like screws, to transmit power from the motors to the joints. That design leads to a comparatively fast, powerful arm that still gets the precision advantages of being electrical. The ASEA arms come in a big or little version. The little one is the model IRb-6, which can lift 6 kilograms—about 13.2 pounds. The big one is the model IRb-60, which can lift 60 kilograms—about 132 pounds.

These are a few of the many robot arms. They come in a wide variety of types and are used for a wide variety of jobs,

The little ASEA IRb-6, which can lift about 13 pounds. For a comparison of size, note that the control cabinet is one of the two shown in the photograph of the big ASEA robot. (ASEA Robotics. New Berlin. WI)

all the way from playing chess to moving heavy equipment. In general, each is designed in a way that fits its particular job, so there is plenty of room for robot arms that are intelligent or fast or strong or whatever is needed to do the job.

# 6

# Robots in Space

Robots have existed that carried out their tasks even before robot arms were invented, or robots could roll around in living rooms without bumping into walls. These robots were satellites and probes able to guide their own motions through space, and they're still performing their vital tasks right now.

Whether these unmanned space vehicles are true robots depends on how the word is used. From a strictly scientific point of view, they definitely qualify.

Starting in the late 1950s and continuing ever since, many kinds of robot craft have been sent into space. Among these have been astronomical satellites (orbiting observatories); Surveyor spacecraft that explored the moon, some by orbiting around it, and others by landing on it; the Mariners that orbited Mars and Venus; and the Voyagers that traveled past the distant outer planets and then out of the solar system altogether into interplanetary space. These spacecraft, although they have—depending on their missions—differed from each other in many ways, have certain robotlike characteristics in common: They use sensors to detect their own motions and positions in space, and they take various actions to correct those motions and positions, as needed.

The motion sensors of a space probe are small vibrating weights and spinning gyroscopes. By their own motions, these sensors detect the motions of the space vehicle—just as, even with closed eyes, a person can detect the motions of a car as it turns left or right, or speeds up or slows down. When the spacecraft's onboard computer compares the motions detected with the flight trajectory that the craft was programmed to follow, it can calculate what course errors there are. When a significant error is detected, the computer can order the rocket engines to accelerate or decelerate or swivel into a slightly different direction.

Robot spacecraft also use visual sensors. A pair of telescopes can be set to track two bright objects—such as the sun and the bright star Canopus. This information is used in various ways. For instance, if the sun and the star appear in the correct positions at all times, the computer knows that the spacecraft is "right-side up." Being right-side up in outer space is arbitrary because there is no up or down for a vehicle in orbit around the earth or orbiting through the solar system. However, if the probe's mission requires that it point various scientific instruments in a certain direction to obtain data on some planet, then it matters very much whether or not the probe is "right-side up." If the onboard computer notices that the sun and Canopus are in the wrong places according to the data stored in computer memory, then the computer knows that something is wrong and that, perhaps, the probe is "upside down" or tilted at a wrong angle. The computer orders corrections in this kind of situation by operating onboard gas jets or flywheels that will tilt the probe back into a correct orientation.

Robotic satellites and space probes were using computer logic to govern their own actions long before robot arms and robot vehicles began to go into operation in scientific laboratories and factories on the ground. They were on missions that would have been impractical for humans to undertake. Even though astronauts have now gone on many such voyages, that's an expensive and difficult way to explore space.

Robot spacecraft are often more practical—they don't need food to eat or water to drink or air to breathe or as much special protection from heat and cold and extreme accelerations and other hazards of space as humans do. Robots were needed in space before they were needed on earth, and so they were developed early in the history of robotics.

Some space vehicles were complete robots in every sense of the word, even to having arms and wheels. Among these were the Viking Landers I and II that were sent to Mars to search for microscopic life.

A model of the Viking Lander, shown as it would appear on the surface of Mars, testing the surface for signs of life. (NASA/JPL)

The Viking Landers arrived on the Martian surface in 1976. Each was equipped with an arm that was a sort of shovel able to scoop up samples of Martian soil. The robot was designed to put the soil sample into a small onboard laboratory chamber where experiments were performed to see if the sample contained microscopic life.

In one test, the Lander pumped carbon dioxide into the test chamber. Carbon dioxide is the most plentiful gas in the Martian atmosphere, so it made sense to suppose that any Martian life would breathe carbon dioxide—as plant life does on our planet. However, a slightly radioactive version of carbon dioxide was used in the Martian experiment. After the soil sample was exposed to this radioactive gas, the gas was pumped out of the test chamber and the soil was pulverized. If the soil contained microorganisms, and if those organisms inhaled the radioactive carbon dioxide, then the pulverized sample should release that gas. Because of its radioactivity, the gas could be detected with radiation sensors.

Unfortunately, neither of the two Landers registered any radioactive carbon dioxide after the soil sample was pulverized. Other tests, some involving adding water to the Martian soil to revive possibly dried-out life forms, also failed to show the presence of any living things. A pair of cameras mounted on each of the Viking Landers sent back photos of the surrounding landscape. These photos were designed to show scientists close-ups of the Martian surface, and, it was hoped, larger living things. Again, the results were disappointing. No living things appeared in the photos.

So the search was inconclusive, leaving the question of life on other planets a mystery. But from a robotic standpoint, it was an impressive achievement. The two Viking Landers used onboard intelligence to control their own landings on the Martian surface, with no human supervision. Once landed, they were able to carry out sophisticated experiments, far away from any person, more than a hundred million miles from Earth. They were able to use radiation sensors and cameras and to operate their shovellike arms and conduct their experiments on that distant planet. Lander II continued to transmit data to Earth for four years before losing power in 1980. Lander I kept operating intermittently, sending updated reports to Earth for seven years until it failed in 1983.

Research has been carried out at the Jet Propulsion Laboratory (JPL) of the California Institute of Technology for a more advanced probe—the JPL Rover. This robot would not only land on Mars or some other planet but also would travel across the surface on wheels, using its sensors and intelligence to avoid bumping into obstacles or falling into pits, to examine many different parts of the planetary surface. On Mars, perhaps some other part of the planet will show traces of present-day or past life—or perhaps some other important discoveries remain to be made there. JPL's two Viking Landers looked at only a few square yards of Martian surface. The Rover would be able to wander far.

An artist's conception of the JPL Rover. (NASA/JPL)

If government funding is provided at some future time for JPL Rovers, they will certainly be among the most advanced robots ever used. They will have the intelligence to land on a planet, wander there, carry out experiments, and report their results back to Earth.

# 7

# A Sentry Robot

A robot named "Robart" probably has more sensors than any other robot in the world. Its designer, H. R. Everett of Springfield, Virginia, built the robot to act as a sentry. Robart can patrol a household while its owners are asleep or away on a trip, and can watch out for many kinds of problems.

Robart has no arms and doesn't need any. It patrols a home to detect fire, flood waters, burglars, and many other possible dangers. When it comes across a problem, there are various things it can do, depending on what its sensors detect.

Robart, 5'2" tall and weighing 80 pounds, rolls around the home from room to room on three wheels to make sure everything is secure. Its patrol route is random: There is no way to know which room it will go into next. This unpredictable behavior is good for preventing burglars from breaking in. If Robart had a predictable patrol pattern, a burglar who somehow found out what that pattern was might fool the system by breaking into a room Robart had just left, knowing that the robot wouldn't be back for several minutes. However, Robart might go into the same room two or three times in a row or might go anywhere in the house at any time.

Robart has an amazing number of sensors. Three of these are used to detect fire. The robot has a smoke detector, a thermometer to detect high temperature, and an infrared detector to detect heat waves from a fire. When its sensors signal that there is a fire, Robart sets off an alarm. The robot can also be programmed to turn on a sprinkler to help put out the fire.

Robart also has several sensors to let it know when a burglar has broken in. It discovers the intruder by sound detection or by sensing a change in the pattern of light and shadow, showing that something is moving through the room. Once the robot "sees" that sign of motion, it can turn spotlights on the moving shape and watch it wherever it goes.

When Robart detects a burglar, it reacts the way it does to a fire: It sounds an alarm. But there are other things it does to cope with the burglar. For instance, Robart might be programmed to use its voice to warn the intruder to leave. It can also send out high energy ultrasonic waves so intense that an intruder would become confused or even nauseated.

Robart has many other functions. It has a sensor that detects water on the floor to let it know if the house is flooded, a toxic gas sensor to check for gas leaks from the stove, a seismic vibration sensor to detect earthquakes, and weather sensors to provide storm warnings.

Robart can talk about whatever it senses, using its speech synthesis circuits. It announces, out loud, whether it has detected a flood or a fire or some other danger—whatever it is.

The robot also has sensors to keep it from bumping into furniture, running into walls, and getting into trouble as it makes its rounds. There are several sensors involved in this. Robart has six 8-spring "feelers" that act like a cat's whiskers to sense objects in its path. Robart also uses sonar transmitters and receivers (like a submarine) to avoid collisions. Finally, if these protections fail, it has bumpers (like a car's), and sensors that tell it when a bumper hits against something. Using the information from these sensors, Robart's microprocessors steer it into courses that allow it to go away from or around the obstacles.

Robart, the sentry robot . . .          coming closer . . .

. . . and closer. (H. R. Everett)

Robart can detect the condition of its own batteries. When the batteries are getting low, the onboard microprocessor starts a "docking routine." This takes Robart (like the robot tortoises in Chapter 3) on a course leading to a battery-charging station. In the case of Robart, this station is a little tower about the same height as the robot. Robart follows a beacon to the tower and gets recharged.

Robart has several other sensors and capabilities. This robot is a rolling collection of sensors and artificial intelligence; and it may be the forerunner of even more advanced sentry robots that can watch over homes, buildings, and someday, even city streets.

# 8

# Arms, Wheels, and Legs

The JPL Rover is one example of a robot with an arm and wheels. It has to have both because its planetary mission requires it to dig and to travel. In general, robots that have both arms and wheels are scarce, most robots being specialized as arm-types or wheel-types.

However, there are exceptions. One of these is Timel. Another is a robot named "Avatar," built by Charles Balmer, an experimenter from Ohio. This is an all-around robot, one that has sensors and speech capabilities. It's also interesting looking and really does resemble a robot from a science-fiction film. In an article he wrote for the magazine Robotics Age, Charles Balmer said that a robot, in addition to being a tool and an experiment, is a piece of "imaginative sculpture." He added that "one of the great pleasures in designing and building a robot is to let your imagination run wild." The result of this creative interest on the part of its designer was a robot that looks like some sort of extraterrestrial space traveler carrying a life-support package on its back. Actually, the "pack" on Avatar's back is its computer.

Even Avatar's name was chosen for a particular reason. Since Avatar was designed to be able to hear and recognize human speech, it was important to give the robot a name it could understand easily. Balmer chose "Avatar" because that

Avatar carrying a toolbox. What looks like a backpack is actually Avatar's onboard computer. Notice, also, the key in the robot's belly that operates an on-off switch. (Charles Balmer, Jr.; photograph by Lensart Photography)

word is made up of sounds that would be easy for the robot to recognize. Many different names would have had the right kinds of sound combinations. Balmer happened to pick this one from the name of a character in a movie.

Avatar can recognize thirty command words and can also be trained to take these commands from several different speakers. Furthermore, it can detect which of those speakers is talking to it at any time. The robot can also talk, and its speaking vocabulary is larger than its listening vocabulary. (It is easier to design electronic circuits to say words than to design circuits for understanding words.) Avatar can use four hundred words when it talks.

The 30-inch tall Avatar is well equipped to detect obstacles as it travels around on its three wheels. To begin with, it has a flashing light mounted on the front of its base that causes reflections from walls and objects in its path. These reflections are detected by four light sensors inside a red glass case high on the robot's chest. Avatar's logic steers it away from obstacles that its light sensors detect. But as an extra precaution, it has bumper detectors and acceleration sensors; in case it fails to avoid something it has seen, then these extra sensors tell it that it has bumped into something, and the onboard computer charts a new route to get it away from the obstacle.

Avatar also has light detectors that point downward to alert it to any drops, such as staircases. If it detects a place where it might fall, it avoids that too. As its inventor says, "This prevents the robot from sneaking through an open door and careening down the basement stairs."

Avatar is a two-armed robot. The right arm, with its gripper hand, is used for picking up objects and has 6 degrees of freedom. It can lift a 3-pound weight when stretched out to its full 2-foot length.

Avatar's left arm is used to hook into a power supply when the robot follows a beacon to go back to its home "oasis" for recharging its batteries. The oasis is a low-voltage charging station, and the robot sends a signal to the oasis to turn on its beacon whenever the onboard batteries are getting low. Avatar's logic then sends it toward the beacon. Once it arrives at the oasis, it uses the main beacon and a smaller beacon to find the charging socket. It automatically plugs itself into the socket for its recharge, turns off the beacons, and (as soon as it is completely charged) goes back out to continue its programmed journey.

Another robot with both wheels and arms is a very small tabletop robot named "Quester." Quester is an example of what an experimenter can do working with very simple materials. It is only 8 inches high, more block shaped than human shaped, just as long as it is high, and looks like what it is—a small walking computer. Its outer shell is mostly wood,

Quester (Copyright 1982 ROBOTICS AGE, INC.; reprinted by permission)

with an ironed-on plastic covering designed for model airplanes. Quester's single arm has only one degree of freedom (up and down). But as the robot travels from place to place, the arm can be positioned above an object, then lowered down so that the gripper hand can grab the object. Then the arm raises, and Quester carries the object back to wherever its program directs it. This arm, by the way, is made of wood and paper clips.

Quester was created in England by David L. Buckley, who designed the robot to operate in an area surrounded by black walls. The objects the robot picks up and the obstacles it goes around are white, so that they are easily visible against the black background. Buckley built six pairs of eyes into the tiny robot, three on each side. Each pair is composed of two different kinds of eye. One eye in the pair is a wide-viewing type that just registers the light level on that side of the robot. The second eye in each pair is directional and is designed to pick up bright reflections from the white objects in order to find the objects that it has to pick up and to go around obstacles in its way.

Will robots on wheels ever be replaced by robots on legs? In science-fiction books and films, robots usually walk on legs. In the Star Wars movie trilogy, C-3PO is a legged walker, as are the strange gigantic war machines of the galactic empire. But so far, most real robots aren't walkers, they're rollers.

For the sake of a more interesting story, fictional robots often have legs to make them more like people. However, in reality, walking machines are much harder to build than rolling machines and the possibilities of building vehicles with legs are just starting to be explored.

Scientists Marc Raibert and Ivan Sutherland, working at Carnegie Mellon University, have made some progress in building vehicles with legs. One of the vehicles is a six-legged crawling machine steered by a human driver. The other is a one-legged hopping machine, a sort of computerized pogo stick. The hopper is also hand-controlled—not by someone riding on it but by remote control.

Because they are operated by people, instead of being self-operating, these walking and hopping machines aren't true robots. However, they wouldn't work at all if they weren't also microprocessor controlled. Microprocessors coordinate the motions of the crawling machine's six legs so that the driver can concentrate on steering. Keeping track of the leg motions would be hopelessly complicated for the driver. And on the hopping machine, sensors send signals to onboard microprocessors, telling them whether the machine is out of balance and in what direction. To get the hopper back in balance, the microprocessors respond far faster than the person could ever do at the remote controls.

These crawling and hopping machines are on their way to becoming robots. Humans handle the higher-level tasks such as steering, but microprocessors handle the details. These machines are an important step on the way to robots that can walk or run or jump.

Some robot researchers have already taken the next step and built experimental models of walking robots. One exam-

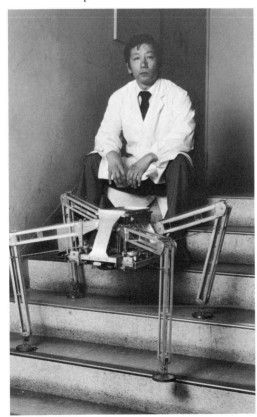

Professor Shigeo Hirose watches his robot climb the stairs. (© Malcolm Kirk )

ple is a four-legged robot built by Professor Shigeo Hirose of the Tokyo Institute of Engineering. His robot is essentially a metal box full of electronic parts with four big metal legs that have knee joints and podlike feet. This robot can walk up and down stairs, using touch sensors in its pods to feel its way along and to adjust its knee joints to move to the next step. Also, a balance sensor in its body keeps the body level during its travels. Professor Hirose's walking robot is only a beginning. A robot with both legs and arms, able to walk from place to place to carry out tasks, will represent the next major step.

There is a real advantage to a walking robot, even outside science fiction. It can go into rough terrain, up staircases, over holes or curbs or boulders in ways that a machine with wheels or even tractor treads couldn't do. Because of those advantages and because of the advances being made by researchers, walking robots are probably coming, and in not very many years.

# 9

# Robots for Fun

As we have seen, hobbyists have been at the forefront of developing and exploring new ideas in robotics. In some cases, imaginative inventors have taken an existing toy "robot" that was not really a robot at all and have added logic to it to make it into a real robot.

One of these inventors is Don McAllister, and the toy he worked with was an R2-D2 built by Kenner Toys, who modeled the toy on the perky little robot from Star Wars. The R2-D2 toy is radio controlled. It is sent radio commands, which it receives on a built-in antenna, telling it to stop or go and which way to turn. By the operation of push buttons on a control box, R2-D2 can be sent anywhere as long as it has a smooth surface to travel over, such as a linoleum floor or a tabletop. But as originally built, it isn't a robot. It only looks like one. It can't be programmed and has no sensors and no decision-making abilities of its own.

McAllister bought one of these toys and set to work to make it into a real robot. The first thing he did was to mount two sensors on it. One of these was a light detector, the other a touch sensor. Although this R2-D2 had a radio receiver, it had no transmitter. McAllister attached a long wire to it so that its sensors could send signals to McAllister's computer, a Tandy Radio Shack TRS-80. Then he connected the computer to R2-D2's control box so that the computer could take over the robot's motions. At that point, McAllister had a real robot and was able to program it to find its way around in a tabletop world, going toward lights and avoiding obstacles—much like other experimental robots.

Another robot builder, Mark Robillard, also adapted a toy robot to make it real. But instead of working with a traveling robot, he chose a toy robotic arm. The arm was the Armatron built by Tomy Toys. Robillard observed that the toy manufacturers often use very good mechanical designs for their "robots," solving many of the engineering problems that a robot designer would have to deal with. Therefore, he concluded that a toy robot was often a good starting point for an experimenter. He saw that Armatron had a very well-designed arm with 5 degrees of freedom and a gripping hand. It could lift a weight of 8 ounces with the arm extended to its full 12-inch length and could also bend back to pick up objects next to its base.

The toy was designed to be operated by a person who would use two joysticks to control the arm motions. Robillard felt that the joystick controls were so well designed that there was no point in taking the toy apart to replace them with computer controls. Instead, he decided to replace himself—that is, replace the person who would operate the joystick. So he built a rig that included some simple computer-driven motors that would move the joysticks. His computer-driven motors were really a second robot that operated the Armatron controls.

It may sound at first as if the inventor, in building one robot to operate another robot, was doing things the hard way. However, the motors he used to move Armatron's joysticks were much simpler than Armatron's arm. In other words, he built a very simple robot to operate the existing precision arm.

With inventors taking this kind of interest in making toy

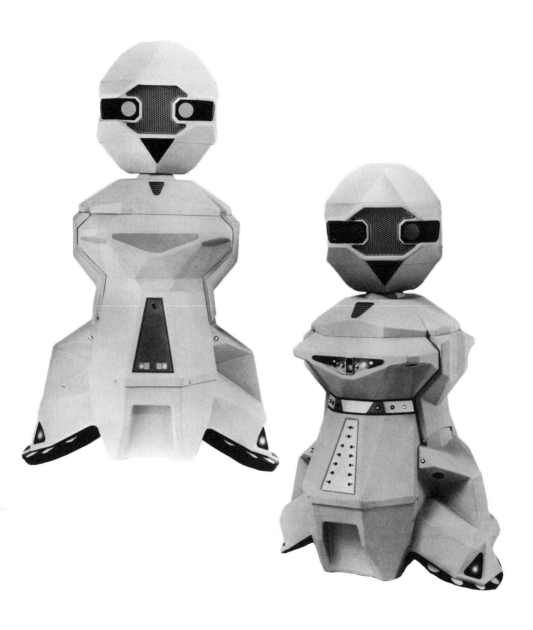

Topo and B.O.B., also known as "Brains on Board." (© 1983 Androbot. Inc.)

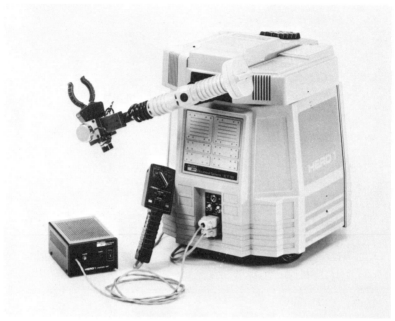

Above: Hero I (Heath Company) Below: The insides of Hero I, showing programming keys. (Heath Company)

robots real, it was only a matter of time before someone would build a real robot that was intended, from the start, for entertainment. Several robot builders have done this.

One example is Androbot, a company in Sunnyvale, California. Androbot has produced two home robots. One of these is Topo, which takes orders from a personal computer. The second is B.O.B. (which stands for "Brains On Board"), a robot that has built-in intelligence and doesn't need an external computer. Both these robots are designed to roam around a home, talking to people or bringing them refreshments.

B.O.B. has ultrasonic sensors so that it can measure the locations of walls as well as chairs, tables, and other objects in the room. Then it uses this information to navigate without bumping into things. The robot also has infrared sensors that detect people by their body heat. So B.O.B. can tell a person from a chair and can use this information to go up to people, talk to them (using a speech synthesizer), or bring them things.

Another robot designed for personal use is the Hero 1 from the Heath Company in Benton Harbor, Michigan. This is a wheeled robot with a gripping arm and the ability to talk, using a speech synthesizer. Its sensors allow it to detect sound, light, and motion. Hero 1 is specifically designed for someone who wants to learn about robotics. It is built in a way that gives an experimenter easy access to printed circuit boards and other parts of the system, and a training course comes with it. This is a robot for someone who wants to experiment on a robot, reprogram it, or take it apart, modify it, and put it back together again. In fact, a hobbyist can buy Hero in kit form and assemble the robot at home.

Still another household robot is one named "Ahmad," built by Donald Dixon in Milpitas, California, for use in his own home. Donald Dixon not only gave Ahmad a voice, but he also gave the robot a human-looking face—a painted plastic mask modeled on his own face and filled with liquid rubber. Ahmad, looking more like a human than do most robots, was built from such easy-to-get parts as coffee cans and coat hangers. Dixon's wife, Ann, supplied some clippings of her own hair for the robot's eyebrows.

Ahmad's main job was to help the builder and his wife watch over their two children, who were one and two years old when Ahmad was built. The robot would not only entertain the children but would also let their parents know where they were in the house.

# 10

# Robots at Work

Among the most advanced robots in existence are those used as industrial arms to carry out jobs in factories. Often, the jobs they are given are dangerous or exhausting or very monotonous for humans. Robots have been installed in factories in several countries to do such tasks as spray-painting, welding, and moving parts from place to place in a manufacturing plant.

Some robots are being used to help build computers, so that, in a way, they are participating in operating the very industry that produced them. For example, a company called Zehntel, Inc., is using a robot arm to assemble computer systems. The arm, a Model 605 manufactured by Intelledex, inserts electronic circuit boards into "card cages." Like the MiniMover and TeachMover robots of Chapter 4, the Intelledex 605 uses stepper motors, unusual for an advanced industrial arm.

One way to tell when a robot is using stepper motors is by sound—steppers make a high-pitched noise as they turn on and off. Furthermore, as the arm joints change their speeds from moment to moment, the mixed sounds from the different steppers change pitch. So, when you watch a robot of this kind go through its motions, you typically hear a soft, rather random musical sound like someone in the distance learning to play bagpipes.

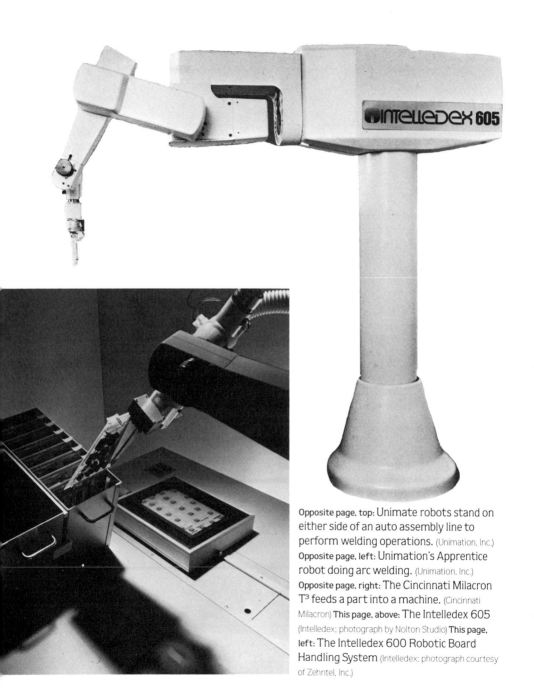

Opposite page, top: Unimate robots stand on either side of an auto assembly line to perform welding operations. (Unimation, Inc.) Opposite page, left: Unimation's Apprentice robot doing arc welding. (Unimation, Inc.) Opposite page, right: The Cincinnati Milacron T³ feeds a part into a machine. (Cincinnati Milacron) This page, above: The Intelledex 605 (Intelledex; photograph by Nolton Studio) This page, left: The Intelledex 600 Robotic Board Handling System (Intelledex; photograph courtesy of Zehntel, Inc.)

There are many other examples of robots used in industry. For instance, at Northrop Aircraft in El Segundo, California, a $T^3$ robot works with other robots to build layers of a plasticlike material (actually made of a woven graphite fiber) to make lightweight hulls for fighter aircraft. The operation is carried out by a whole roomful of robots whose actions are coordinated by a central computer.

First, rolls of the dark fabric are automatically spread out on a cutting table and cut into separate shapes like pieces of a huge jigsaw puzzle. The cutting operation is done by a computer-controlled knife machine. Next, three robotic carts, traveling on overhead rails, pick up removable table sections with the fiber shapes on them. The carts travel along their rail system to take these table sections to a working surface on the floor in front of the $T^3$ robot.

The $T^3$ has to pick up the thin pieces of fiber sheet and build them into layers on another cart at floor level near the working surface. In order to pick up the thin fabric sections, the $T^3$ has been fitted with several vacuum hoses that make it look like a gigantic octopus looming over the work area. Its program tells it exactly where to reach to pick up each section and where to put it on the waiting cart. When the cart has been loaded, it rolls out of the robotic work area to go to a furnace, where the layers of woven graphite are heated into a hard section of material, which is later fitted into place as part of an aircraft fuselage.

The $T^3$ is a very strong robotic arm and also is very precise. It can be programmed in many details of its motion—not only involving what it picks up and where it moves it but also such details as how fast it should move. The hand end of the robot arm can be programmed to move at any speed from 1 inch a second (about the speed of a crawling ant) to more than 10 feet a second. Like TeachMover, this large arm—bigger than a human being—can be led through a detailed routine by a human operator at a control panel, and, in going through the

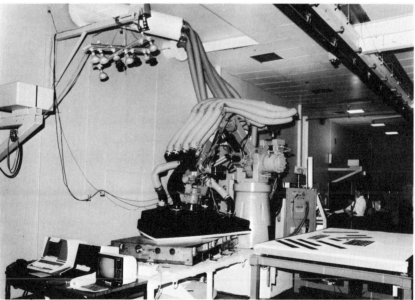

Above: The $T^3$ robot, equipped with a special vacuum head, hovers above the work table like a huge octopus. (Cincinnati Milacron; photograph courtesy of Northrop Corporation) Below: Here the $T^3$ has moved selected sheets of graphite to a new position on a different surface. This photograph shows part of the overhead rail system that is used by robot carts to bring materials to the $T^3$. (Cincinnati Milacron; photograph courtesy of Northrop Corporation)

routine, will learn all the steps. Then it will be able to do the job itself.

Robots built for work in industry have to be able to work very exactly because they are usually doing tasks (such as helping in the manufacture of airplanes) that must be done precisely right. Also, a powerful robot can cause a great deal of damage if anything goes wrong with its operation. In one incident, the control unit for a robot working in an experimental laboratory at the University of Florida burned out. The suddenly mindless robot kept pounding its arm against its supporting stand until it tore off its own shoulder and reduced itself to scrap. A graduate student working with the system stood well out of the way while this was going on.

A robot placing a bolt into a metal part is likely to smash right through the metal part if the hole isn't where the robot thought it was. Research has been carried out at the Jet Propulsion Laboratory of the California Institute of Technology on the problems a robot faces in performing the simple act of putting a bolt into a hole.

A metal part with two holes in one side is used as the target. The shape of this part is programmed into the memory of a computer that controls a television camera and a robot arm. Also programmed into the system's memory is the ability to recognize the shape of the part and the locations of the holes as seen by the TV camera.

As the camera views the room, the computer sends commands to the robot arm, directing it to aim the bolt at the hole. In other words, this computer uses both an eye (the camera) and an arm to do its task.

However, the computer's use of the TV picture is not very exact. It's only good enough for the arm to get the bolt close to the hole. This is understandable if you imagine yourself trying to tell a blindfolded person at the opposite end of a room exactly where to aim a bolt to get it into a hole.

So the system is also given a sense of touch. The robot

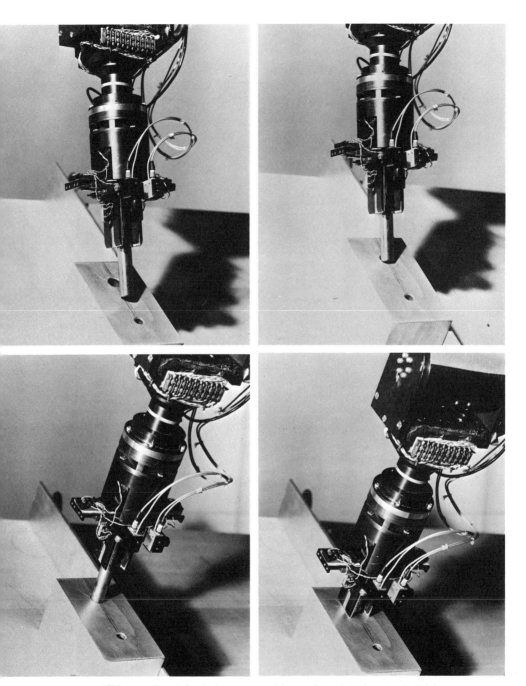

JPL's experimental robot arm uses vision and touch to insert a bolt into a hole. (NASA/JPL)

arm is programmed to approach the target at an angle. As soon as touch sensors on the arm detect the fact that the bolt is pressing against the target object, the computer issues new commands, telling the arm to slide the bolt in the direction of the selected hole. Then, when the arm feels the bolt slide partway into the hole, the computer orders it to shift to a straight approach. Finally, the arm pushes the bolt all the way into the hole.

Robot arms aren't the only active robots in industry. Robot carts are also used to transport materials from place to place in factories.

The carts use electronic sensors to follow wires buried under the factory floor. An electronic controller, which is a small, specialized computer, sends signals through the buried wires, and the robots sense these signals. When a robot comes to a branch in the buried wire, it will go in the same direction the electronic signal goes at that branch. So the controller is acting like a switch on a model railroad—except that in this case, the rails are invisible to all but the robot carts.

The carts also have bumpers and feelers like cat whiskers to tell them when they have bumped into or are scraping against something. When this happens the cart stops until someone corrects the situation.

The loads these carts carry are held overhead, sometimes by robot arms or in small cranes. When the cart arrives at a location under the load it is supposed to pick up, the controller, operating from a distant part of the factory, turns off the signal running through the buried wire, and the cart stops. Then the controller orders the cart to raise its platform. The platform rises until the load is resting on it. At this point the robot arm or crane lets go of the load, and the cart goes rolling away again, carrying the load to its new destination, where another arm will take it off. J. F. Derry, the author of an article in Robotics Age magazine about these carts, says they look like "a herd of turtles whizzing about on wheels with boxes on their backs."

The Automated Systems Division of Bell & Howell, in Zeeland, Michigan, takes a different approach to robotic carts. Instead of following buried wires, Bell & Howell's AGV (automatic guided vehicle) uses a visual sensor to trace a fluorescent chemical pathway invisible to people. Pattern variations in the fluorescent path tell the robot where to stop. The pathway has the advantage of being usable on concrete, tile, carpeting, and other kinds of surfaces. Also, the path can be erased chemically and redrawn to give the carts new routes.

The Bell & Howell intelligent AGV (automatic guided vehicle). (Bell & Howell, Inc.)

The AGVs carry onboard computers with keyboards for programming and reprogramming. Also, a central computer sends FM radio signals to the carts. Combined with its path-tracking capability, this gives the robot cart three levels of intelligence. The AGVs can open closed doors, ride elevators, give commands for loading or unloading machines, give flashing or chiming signals, and avoid collision with other robot carts.

# 11

# The Future of Robots

Robots will probably develop at a fantastic rate over the coming years, just because the computer technology they depend on is developing so fast. Today's robots are very far ahead of those that existed ten or twenty years ago. And forty years ago, they would have been considered pure fantasy. People then had no idea of the amazing technological strides that were coming. It's just as impossible for us to know what robots will be like in another ten or twenty or forty years, especially since advances are happening faster all the time.

Some kinds of developments seem very likely. For instance, the ability to speak and to hear and understand speech is evolving rapidly now in computer systems. It is a good guess that our computers and robots will be able to hold intelligent conversations with us in a few years from now. And it's also a good guess that robots will be cheaper, and much more flexible and versatile—able to do a wide variety of simple tasks. By the turn of the twenty-first century, it may be commonplace to tell a robot to go downstairs and bring back a certain book. The ability to select the right book, by the way, would be a result of computer developments in visual recognition, including the ability to read and recognize letters and numbers. So you could tell your robot the name of the book you wanted, and you might make its search easier by telling the robot what color and size book to look for.

Some of the anticipated uses for robots will be coming fairly soon. The employment of robots in harsh environments such as outer space, undersea, deserts, or Arctic and Antarctic climates will be increased. For instance, a robot is being planned that will be able to repair communications or weather satellites in orbit. The repair robot will be launched by a manned space shuttle and will dock in space with the faulty satellite to carry out its repair operations, using sophisticated sensors and manipulating arms and a very advanced computer program.

Robots will be used increasingly in helping human workers on dangerous or monotonous jobs. We may see robot firefighters, robot bridge painters, robots that investigate and disarm bombs, and robots that clean up dangerous chemical spills. Robot sentries, representing improvements on Robart, will stand guard in homes and businesses.

Robots on wheels will have greater uses, doing more mail-delivery jobs inside large companies and (somewhat further in the future) doing delivery jobs along city and town streets.

Research and development is going on now to develop robots that will help handicapped people. Someone who is confined to a wheelchair or bed will be able to operate a push-button control box to have a robot fetch things and assist in various ways. The handicapped person will also be able to speak to the robot to give it orders. And these same kinds of robots will eventually be available to help everyone.

Much of the improvement in robots, making them more intelligent and able to do a wider variety of jobs, will come about as a result of advances in programming languages. Universities, research laboratories, and manufacturers are involved in developing languages particularly suited to robots.

The programming of a robot is what makes it a flexible system, able to do many different kinds of tasks. And the key to giving robots added intelligence and new capabilities lies in finding new ways to program them.

There are several very advanced robotic languages in existence today. Using an advanced language, a programmer can give a precision, industrial robot an exact description of a large number of objects in its work area—including the size, shape, and location of each object, and the angles at which the objects are tilted. Suppose the robot then works on the objects, moving them around. Its program will allow it to recalculate the position of each object after it has been moved. Then, even after a robot arm has moved all the parts from place to place, twisted them around, and worked on them in various ways (perhaps fitting some of them together in an assembly operation), it still can keep track of each object's exact position. The AL language developed at Stanford University, perhaps the most advanced robotic language in use, is particularly good at keeping track of objects in this way.

Another advanced robotic language was developed by International Business Machines Corporation (IBM) for use with its industrial robots. The language is called "AML," which stands for "A Manufacturing Language." In addition to allowing a robot arm to keep track of the positions of objects it is working on, AML can collect data on the robotic operation so that information can be sent to a central computer on how many parts the robot is moving, how fast it is operating, whether it is making errors, and other record-keeping details.

In AL and AML and other advanced robotic languages, the programmer needs to program only the endpoints of an arm's motion—the locations it has to reach in order to pick up something or put it down or do some other particular action. Other program sequences under the control of the robot's computer will calculate the motions the arm has to follow to go smoothly and efficiently from one programmed endpoint to the next.

But in spite of the sophistication of some of these robot languages, they are all limited. Even the most advanced languages use "robot-level" instructions—that is, they have to

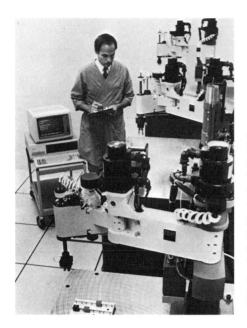

An IBM Personal Computer is being used to program these robots. Each robot, called an "IBM 7535 Manufacturing System," is a jointed arm having four degrees of freedom. The arm in the foreground is working with the parts on the table to do an assembly operation. This is one of several IBM robot models that use a special robotic programming language called "AML." (IBM)

include exact positional information telling the robot where objects are at the beginning of the task.

Suppose a human being needed this same amount of information in order to do a task. If you wanted to ask someone to change a light bulb, you would have to say something like, "The light bulb's center is 3 feet above the floor, 7 feet from the south wall, and 1 foot, 3½ inches from the west wall of this room." You would have to explain the location of a spare bulb in the same kind of exact measurements, along with details on how to twist bulbs to get them in and out of sockets. Instead, a person can simply say, "Would you do me a favor and put a new bulb in the lamp next to the couch? There are some spare bulbs in the top kitchen drawer. . . ."

The future uses of robots will widen enormously if they can be spoken to in that informal way, instead of being told exact measurements. This doesn't mean there would be any need to speak aloud to them—although even that may be possible, as computers continue to develop an ability to respond to spoken commands. But even to be able to enter typed code into a robot's computer to tell it what to do, without having to tell it every single measurement, would make precision robots easier to use. The programmer, instead of having to spend hours programming the locations of objects, could concentrate on programming the facts about the task needed to be done.

Robotic languages with that kind of free style are called "task-oriented languages." As of now, there are no completely developed task-oriented languages. However, research is being done to construct them. An experimental version of such a language was developed by Larry Lieberman, Mike Wesley, and Tomas Lozano-Perez of IBM's Thomas J. Watson Research Center in Yorktown Heights, New York, in the mid-1970s. This language, called "AUTOPASS," was used to instruct a robot to put some simple parts together, using program statements such as "LOWER INTERLOCK TO CONTACT BRACKET."

AUTOPASS was useful as an experiment in task-oriented languages. But it wasn't meant for actual industrial situations and was usable only in a very carefully controlled situation where all the objects it was working with were very precisely placed, and there were no possibilities for error.

The difficulty in creating a task-oriented language has a lot to do with the way software deals with errors. In a robot-level language (with all locations exactly spelled out), after a sensor lets the robot arm know how it is positioned, the robot can calculate how it must change its position to get to the object it is supposed to pick up or work on. But if the robot were using a task-oriented language in which it didn't know the exact locations of objects, it would have to be programmed with very detailed images of the objects it was working with and of the various floor, wall, or bench-top surfaces in the work area so that it could find its way around more or less the way a human being would.

In 1980, Jeanine Meyer (also at IBM in Yorktown Heights) developed a program designed to find solutions to this problem. Her program, named EMULA, instead of being a robot language itself, is a sort of training tool for robot languages—a program that explores the ways in which robot languages can be improved to handle spatial problems.

EMULA displays robot arms and other objects in exact detail on a computer screen. It calculates the motions of a robotic arm as it moves and turns, as it picks up objects; it calculates when the robot arm would bump into things; and it calculates the signals various sensors would send to the robot as light and shadow, obstacles, and other conditions were measured.

The ways in which EMULA creates computerized pictures of the robot work space are known as "world modeling." In effect, EMULA creates a logical model of the robot and its work space. Using EMULA, computer scientists can search for ways to build robot languages with world-modeling capabilities.

When robot languages finally include world modeling, and when they become fully task oriented, precision robots will no longer have to follow orders spelled out in every detail. Instead, they will be able to handle most of the details on their own. Once that is possible, robots could be programmed very quickly and easily to do all sorts of very complex jobs, and people will be able to ask robots to do things almost as naturally as if they were asking other people.

What will life be like, as robots—becoming more intelligent all the time—gradually enter into our world? It depends, as do so many things, on whether we have the sense to use robots wisely. Some serious problems may arise as robots continue taking over the functions they perform with greater strength and efficiency than human beings. If, however, we use them wisely, robots may free us to pursue new opportunities in jobs that call for human understanding, feeling, judgment, and creativity and—above all—the ability of people to communicate. If so, then perhaps we won't lose out after all. This challenge has arisen before in human history, in other forms. The mastery of fire and the invention of the wheel and the bow and arrow in primitive times, and the development of machinery in more recent history, led to major upheavals in the way people lived. Advances in the sciences of physics, chemistry, and biology in our own century have produced tremendous benefits, but have also led to weapons of war more destructive than the world has ever seen before. Robots, creations of the Computer Age, cause us trouble or greatly improve our lives—depending on how we use them.

## Twenty-One-Statement List on Computer Technology

(Note: These twenty-one statements are best read in sequence because each statement builds on previous ones.)

1. **Semiconductor:** Some materials, such as metals, are very good "conductors" of electricity, and electric current flows through them easily, meeting little resistance. Other materials, known as "insulators" or "nonconductors," have considerable resistance to the flow of electricity. Examples include rubber and glass. Some substances, called "semiconductors," are just at the border between being conductors and nonconductors. Silicon, a common mineral found in sand and in many kinds of rock, is an important semiconductor in electronics. Silicon becomes very delicately balanced between the conducting and nonconducting state when small traces of certain impurities are added to it. In this "semiconducting" state, a small triggering signal can shift silicon in either direction.

2. **Doping:** The addition of impurities to silicon is known as "doping." Doping can be done using different kinds of impurities at different levels (the amounts of impurities added). When neighboring sections of a small silicon chip are doped with different impurities or to different levels, that is referred to as "selective doping."

3. **Transistor:** Through certain precise patterns of selective doping, a silicon chip can be made into a "transistor," an electronic switch that can be

switched off and on by very small control signals. A transistor is far smaller and faster than any mechanical switch. Transistors have almost entirely replaced vacuum tubes, light-bulb-like electronic switches that are comparatively big, slow, costly and power consuming. Transistors today can switch between off and on in less than a nanosecond (a billionth of a second).

4. **Integrated circuit:** An integrated circuit (usually called an "IC") is made up of a very large number of microscopic transistors formed on a single silicon chip. A square chip ¼ inch on a side may include hundreds of thousands of transistors. These are connected by a complex network of conducting paths etched onto the chip. The arrangement in which the microscopic transistors are interconnected is referred to as the "architecture" of the chip or of the IC.

5. **Binary logic:** At any given moment, each transistor in an electronic circuit is either off or on. Because of the way transistors are connected to each other on a chip, (and also the way separate IC chips are connected together), when one transistor is switched off or on, other transistors switch off or on, too. In this way, a single switching event can set an entire circuit into action. However, these actions follow a definite pattern, established by the architecture of the chip. The off-or-on conditions of various transistors (as complex a pattern as that of all the lit and unlit windows in a city) can be used as a code to stand for such things as arithmetic operations, the motion or storage of information, or control signals telling still other transistors to switch off or on. The whole pattern of off-on coding is called "binary logic," meaning a logic based on two conditions—in this case, the off-or-on condition of each transistor. Each transistor's off-or-on code is called a "bit" of information.

6. **Memory chip:** A memory chip is one in which the off-or-on conditions of large numbers of transistors are used to stand for stored information. The information can be virtually anything—scientific data, birth records, salaries of employees in a company, weather conditions, and so on. Information stored in memory is usually called "data." An advanced memory chip can store a quarter of a million bits of data.

7. **Microprocessor:** A microprocessor is a chip in which the bit pattern of the transistors stand for logic, control, or arithmetic operations. A certain bit pattern may order data to be moved from one memory location to another; another pattern may call for the addition of two numbers; still another pattern may command some device (such as a printer) to go into operation.

8. **Computer:** A computer is an electromechanical device that can accept input information, operate on that information by using its built-in logic, and produce output results or "answers." There are two kinds of computers—analog and digital.

9. **Analog computer**: An analog computer is a specialized kind of computer that uses signals of varying sizes in the form of electrical currents or voltages to do its calculations. The operation of an analog computer roughly resembles the operation of a car. The acceleration of a car depends on how far the driver presses down on the gas pedal, and the sharpness of a turn depends on how far the driver turns the steering wheel. In a similar way, an analog computer responds to the amounts of current, voltages, and other electrical quantities established, for instance, by the setting of dials. Analog computers are used only in very special applications and play no significant part in present-day robotics.

10. **Digital computer**: A digital computer operates by binary logic. Even though it receives inputs and produces outputs in such varied forms as words, decimal numbers, and diagrams, all of these are handled as combinations of binary offs and ons inside the computer. A digital computer receives data in definite numerical form, somewhat as an elevator does. The elevator passenger presses an exact button to enter an exact number (rather than pressing a pedal "just so far" and turning a wheel "just so far" as the car driver has to do), and the elevator takes the passenger to an exact floor. Most present-day computers are digital computers, which are the basis of present-day robotics. (For the remainder of this list, "computers" will always mean digital computers.)

11. **Central processing unit**: The central processing unit (or "CPU") is the part of the computer that carries out logical, arithmetic, and control functions. It is the center of "intelligence" in the computer. Most of the CPU's intelligence is located in a microprocessor chip. Some CPUs include additional microprocessor chips, called "coprocessors," which take over certain tasks, such as special calculations, and input/output (I/O) control, to unburden the main microprocessor. The CPU also includes memory chips. However, a computer generally includes a main memory, located outside the CPU, where most of the storage is located.

12. **Machine language**: Since, at the most fundamental level, the transistors of a digital computer operate, according to binary logic, in just two conditions (off or on), a simple number code made up of zeros and ones can be used to stand for the condition of an IC at any moment. This language of zeros and ones is known as "machine language" because it matches exactly the offs and ons of the transistors. A 16-bit word in machine language would be a random-looking arrangement like this: 0010 1000 1001 0111. But while it would look random to a casual observer, each word of machine language would have a definite meaning to a computer. The strings of zeros and ones typed by a machine language programmer could be changed automatically into offs and ons by the computer's electronic circuits and could be used to trigger key events inside the CPU and memory.

13. **High-level language:** Many of the most advanced professional computer programmers work in machine language because it is the closest language to the electronic workings of the computer. Machine language plays a big part in the design of IC architecture and in the establishment of the fundamental logic capabilities of a computer. But machine language is complex and is unlike human language, so it is impractical for a user who needs to program a computer to solve certain kinds of problems or handle certain kinds of tasks. To take care of these needs, high-level languages have been developed that use more familiar words, numbers, and symbols. There are hundreds of high-level languages, each designed for certain purposes. A few of the better known of these are FORTRAN (a scientific language), COBOL (a business language), BASIC (a language that emphasizes simplicity and familiar everyday words for ease of use in many applications), Pascal (a language that emphasizes very efficient programming techniques), and LISP (a language designed for experiments in artificial intelligence). Most of these languages come in different variations known as "dialects." BASIC alone includes hundreds of dialects. These languages are used by applications programmers who work more efficiently with a natural language than they could in machine language. Also, a high-level language is much faster for a programmer to work with because each statement in the high-level language can stand for dozens of statements in machine language. However, even in the comparatively simple BASIC, statements are still quite different from conversational English. For instance, here is an example of a statement in BASIC:

55   ON R GOSUB 200, 210, 220

This statement, located at program address 55, tells the computer logic to get its next instruction at program address 200 if a previously calculated quantity, R, equals 1, at program address 210 if R equals 2, and at program address 220 if R equals 3. At each of these addresses, the computer will find different instructions to follow, leading to different results.

14. **Program:** A computer program is a series of coded statements written by a person (a programmer) in a form that tells a computer, step by step, what actions to take. The program generally gives the computer different choices, depending on what inputs it gets (for instance, signals from instruments detecting temperatures, light signals, or other conditions). The computer will also make different choices depending on the results that it gets at each point in its calculations. The line of BASIC shown under item 13 is an example. Earlier in the program, the value of some quantity R was calculated to be either 1, 2, or 3, and now the computer will take a different path through the program for each of those results. The computer always translates the program statements into binary logic—that is, into a pattern of offs and ons for all its thousands of transistors. If a program is written in a high-level language, then another

program called a "compiler" or an "interpreter" is used by the computer to translate the high-level statements into machine language. Finally, each machine language statement is translated into the binary logic of offs and ons.

15. **Artificial intelligence:** Any computer acts, to some extent, intelligent. Its "intelligence" is built into it by its designers and by the programmers who supply it with programs. In a more primitive example, even the builder of a mousetrap puts some intelligence into the mousetrap—an intelligence that says, "Snap if something bumps the catch of the trap, otherwise don't snap." The mousetrap isn't intelligent, but the person who builds it (its designer) and the person who sets it (who is, in a very primitive sense, its programmer) provide the intelligence, leaving that intelligence behind in the trap. Similarly, a computer contains the intelligence of its designers and its programmers in a very complex, fast-acting form, able to solve problems and make decisions at a speed that no person could ever approach. The term "artificial intelligence" is used in relation to highly advanced, sophisticated computers able to do really incredible things, including learning from their past experiences. Whether such a computer could ever become truly "intelligent" the way a person is intelligent is a matter of philosophical debate, with different people having widely differing opinions.

16. **Software:** A written computer program—whether the programmer scrawls it on a scrap of paper in working out the details or has it printed out by an electronically operated printer after it has been entered into the computer—is known as "software." The program is usually entered into the computer for the first time by someone typing at the computer's keyboard. Then it is saved on a magnetic disk or tape, where (still called "software") it is entered into the computer whenever it is needed. A program to be used over and over again by a particular computer is stored on a permanent, unchanging memory chip called a ROM, which is installed in the computer. In this form, the program is said to be stored in "firmware." Like programs, data can also be stored in software or firmware. The words "software" and "firmware" are used to distinguish the programs and data from the electronic circuits and other permanent physical parts of a computer, which are called "hardware"—a hardware far more sophisticated than anything to be found at the corner hardware store.

17. **Printed circuit board:** Also known as a "PCB," a printed circuit board is a hard plastic board on which ICs and other electronic components are interconnected by copper paths to form a complex circuit. The board may even contain several layers of circuitry, one on top of the other (like the layers of some ancient cities discovered by archeologists). PCBs are made in various standard sizes, measuring several inches in length and width. The PCBs are slid into slots in a computer chassis. Some computers use

only one PCB and are called "single-board computers," and others, especially large complex systems, may use many boards.

**18. Peripherals:** There are many devices used by a computer in its operation. Some of these are used to feed programs or data into the computer; examples include keyboards, magnetic disk drives, and magnetic tape drives. The disk and tape drives are also used to store programs and data when the computer is not using them or when the computer is shut down. There are other devices used by a computer to feed results back to the user; examples include video displays and printers. These input/output and bulk memory devices are called "peripherals." Generally, they have to do with people's communications with the computer. No matter how small the chips are where the basic workings of the computer take place, the peripherals cannot drop below certain size limits. Even though they are becoming more compact all the time, the peripherals need to be of a size a person can use. The display screen has to be large enough to print information a person can read; a keyboard has to be large enough to allow a person's fingertips to hit the keys; a printer has to be large enough to print lines of information on sheets of paper of a convenient size for a person to read; and so forth. For these reasons, computer peripherals can't be brought down to the incredibly small sizes of ICs.

**19. Computer system:** A computer system includes the microprocessors and memory chips, the PCBs on which these are mounted, the cabinets that contain the boards, the peripherals needed for input/output and storage, and electrical power supplies. It can also contain many other parts, depending on its intended use. For example, a computer system might include measuring and control instruments to allow it to monitor and control the operations of a chemical plant.

**20. Sensor:** A sensor is a device that detects light, sound, pressure, physical obstructions, temperature, or other conditions. The sensor then sends signals, based on what it has measured, to an electronic instrument or computer.

**21. Robot:** A robot is another example of a computer system, including not only a CPU, memory, and a means of input to receive programs or commands, but also the framework, motors, and possible sensing instruments needed for its particular robotic function. In its behavior, it is a computerized machine that can be programmed to handle tools and other objects or to travel from place to place. Many robots can use signals from sensors to change their actions. These flexible abilities make a robot capable of carrying out tasks with great efficiency—often jobs that are dangerous, boring, or perhaps impossible for a human worker to do.

# Bibliography

Milton, Joyce. Here Come the Robots. New York: Hastings House, 1981. This is an excellent book for beginners: entertaining and informative, with a variety of photographs. It broadens the scope of the subject by including in the category of robots such remote-controlled devices as the UNUMO —or "Universal Underwater Mobot"—used in undersea explorations.

"Mind Machines." In NOVA: Adventures in Science. pp. 206–13. Reading, MA: Addison-Wesley, 1983. This book is based on television documentaries produced by WGBH in Boston. It includes a robotics section under the topic "Mind Machines," which provides good coverage of Shakey and assembly line robots.

Omni, special issue on "The Robot," April 1983. The entire issue is packed with articles and photos of recent robotic developments.

Osborne, Adam. Running Wild: The Next Industrial Revolution. Berkeley, CA: Osborne/McGraw-Hill, 1979. This is a general book, covering many computer-related subjects, and presenting in an easy-to-read style a survey of how the computer age is affecting our world. In particular, Chapter 4, "The Blue-Collar Robot," provides an excellent overview of the robotics field, with varied photographs and diagrams.

Raibert, Marc H., and Sutherland, Ivan E. "Machines That Walk." Scientific American, January 1983, pp. 44–53. This article describes walking machines developed by the authors. The cover of the magazine shows a picture of one of these machines.

"The Robot Revolution." Time, December 8, 1980, pp. 72–83. This article, which was the cover story of the magazine, is an excellent survey of the subject.

Robotics Age. This bimonthly journal provides updates on what is happening in robotics, including the latest designs of professional and amateur robot builders. It was one of the main sources of information for this book.

Safford, Edward L., Jr. The Complete Handbook of Robotics. Blue Ridge Summit, PA: Tab Books, 1978. This book explains how to design and build a robot, but the reader who is interested in more general information can learn a fair amount by skimming through the text while skipping the engineering details. Included are a wide selection of photographs and many interesting facts on the operation of robots. Since it was written a little before the major growth of robotics, this book does not cover a very large number of robot systems. Those that are dealt with, however, are explained thoroughly.

——. Handbook of Advanced Robotics. Blue Ridge Summit, PA: Tab Books, 1982. Like The Complete Handbook of Robotics, this book, which examines a greater number of robot systems, can also be explored to various depths. For the general reader, skimming the photographs and interesting details will provide a good overview of the field.

Walter, W. Grey. "The Imitation of Life." Scientific American, May 1950, pp. 42–45. Dr. Walter describes his robot tortoises.

# Index

# INDEX